I am grateful for the resources of artificial intelligence, an incredible source of inspiration and innovation, with the ability to offer us the opportunity to process information and push the limits of creativity. May this work celebrate the collaboration between human mind and machine, thanking AI for driving the progress of knowledge.

Sol Machado
2024

Test color page

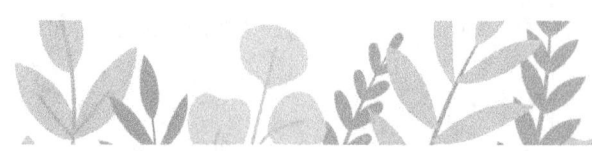
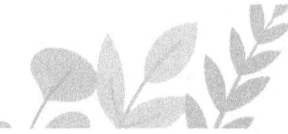

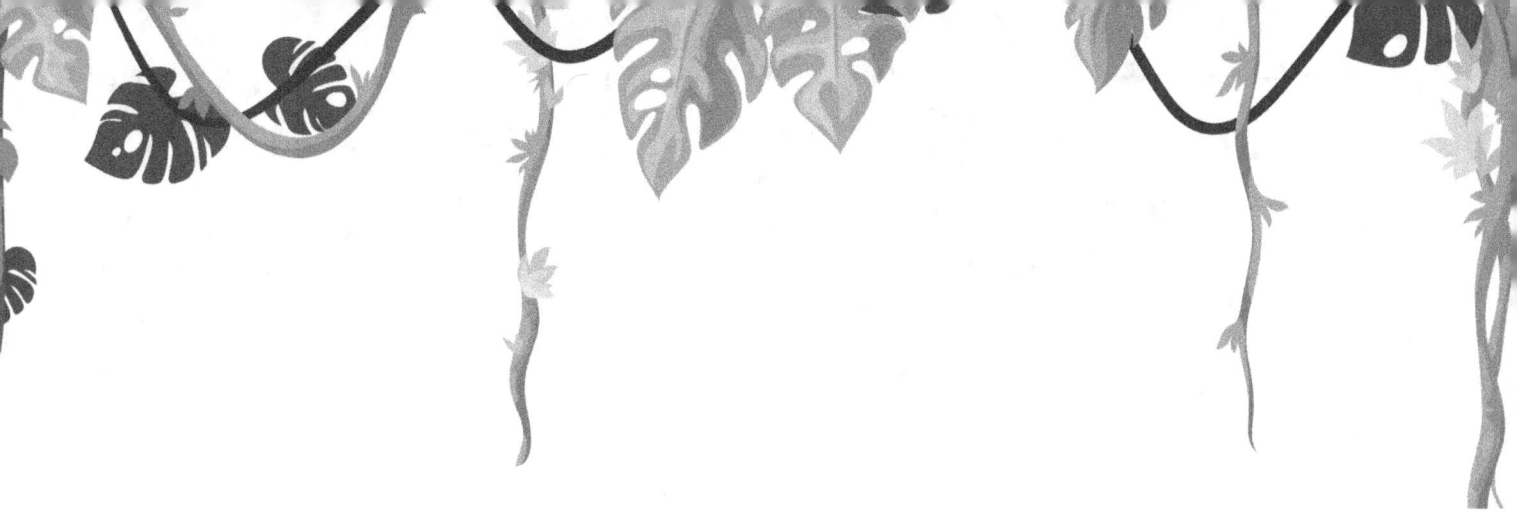

This book belongs to

....

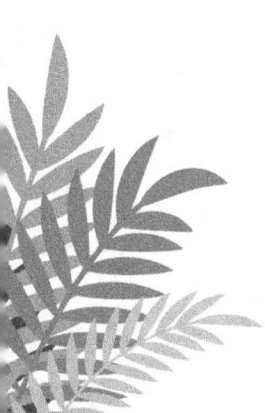

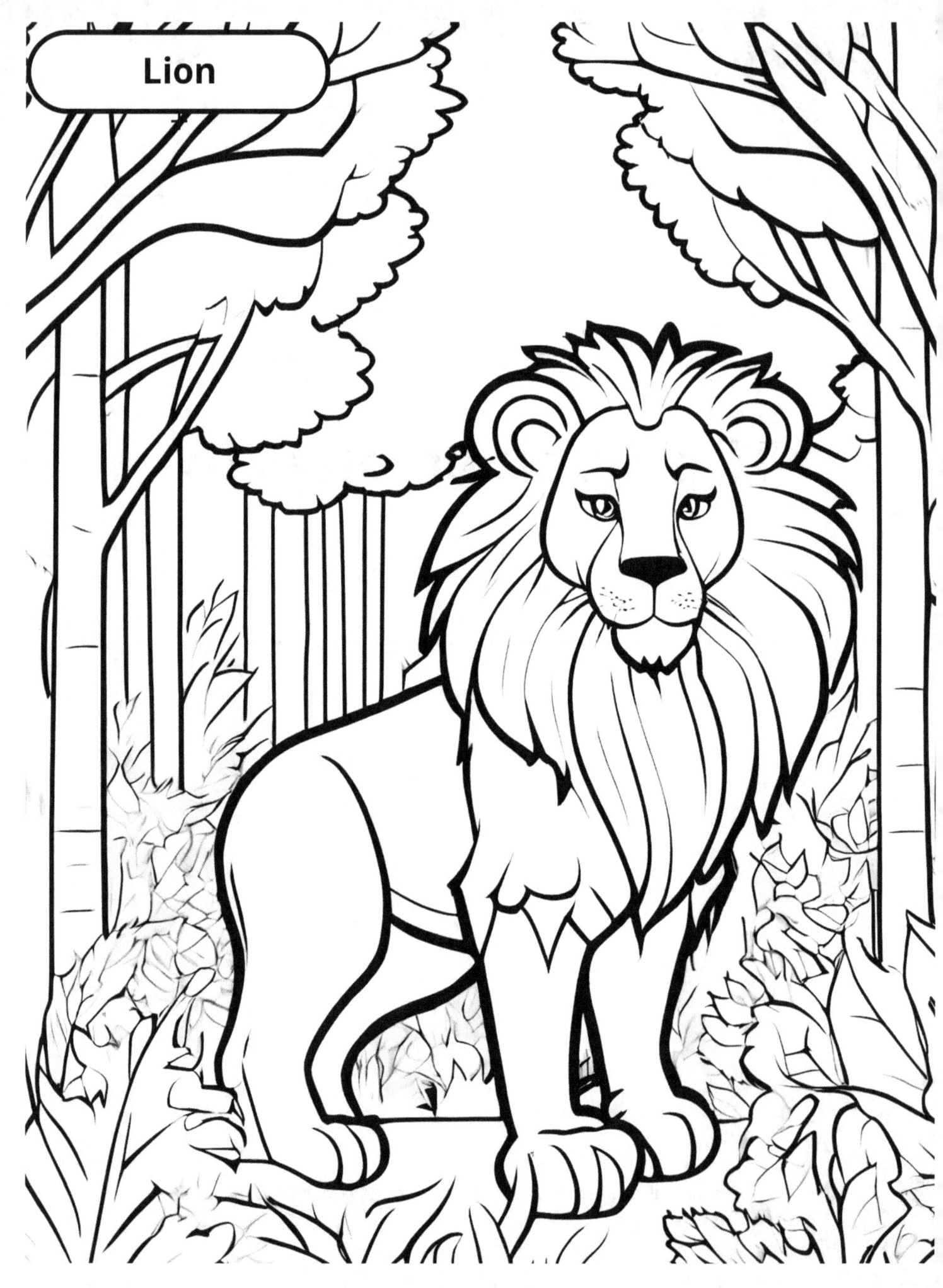

Lion

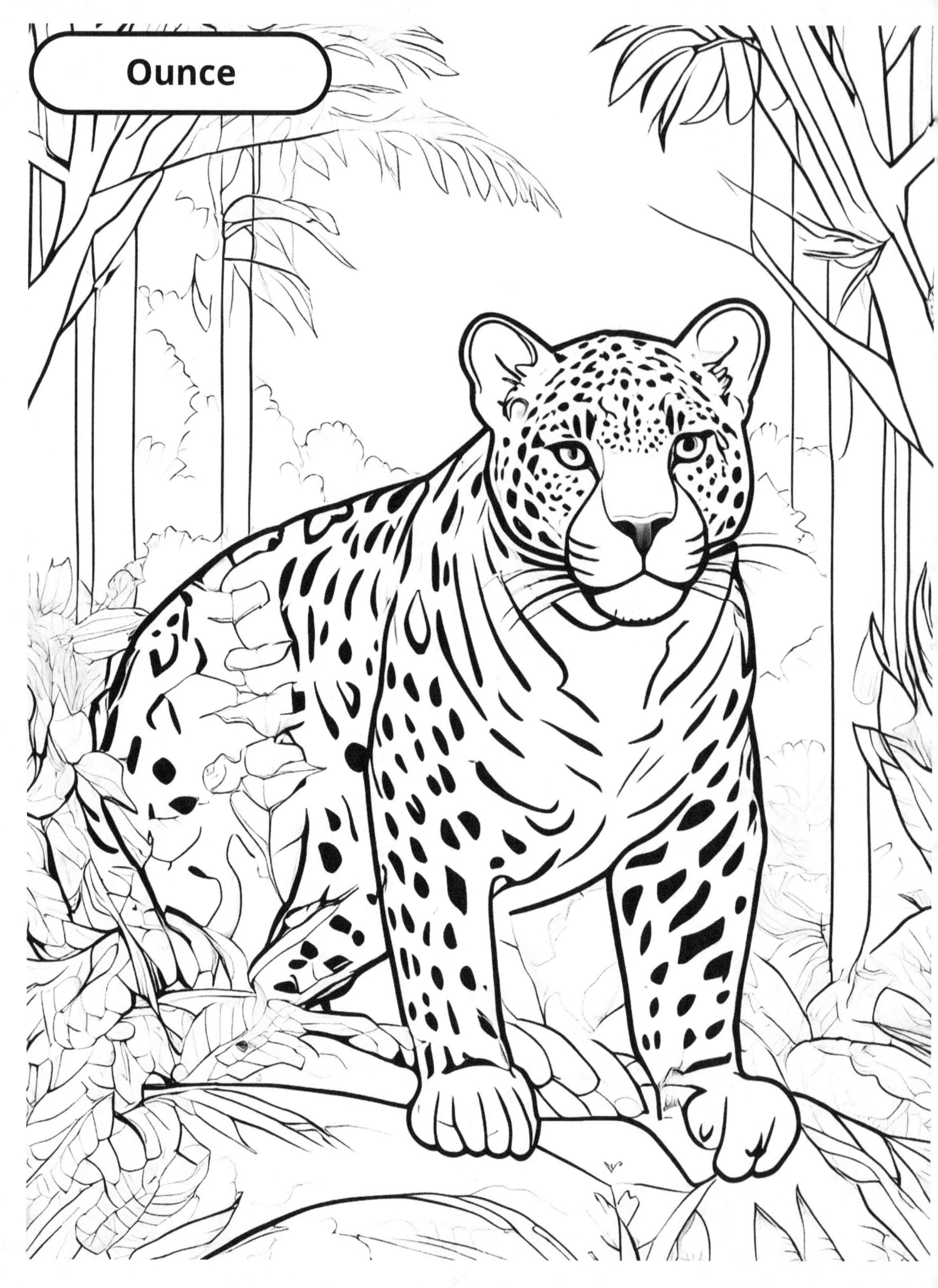

Ounce

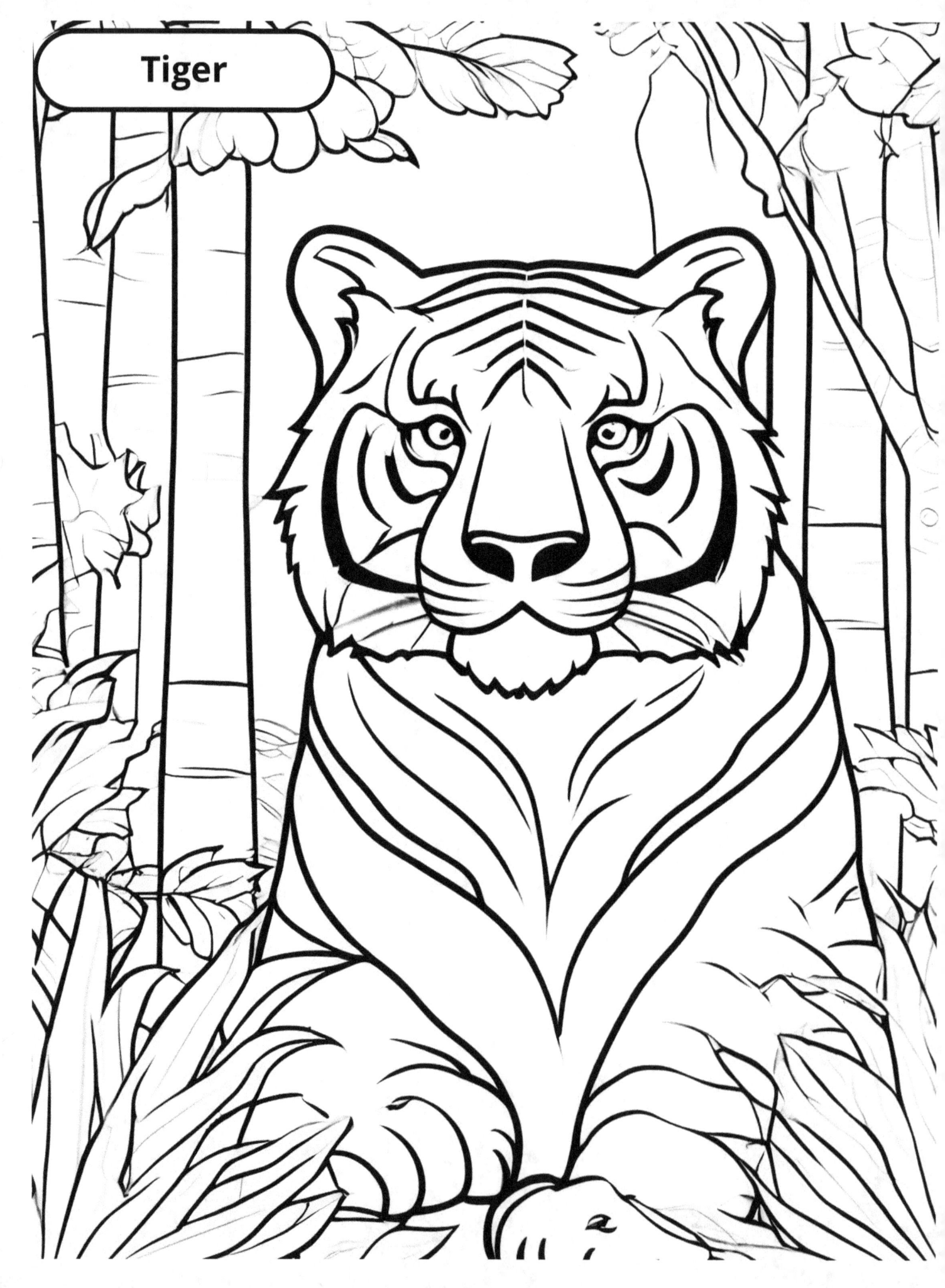

Tiger

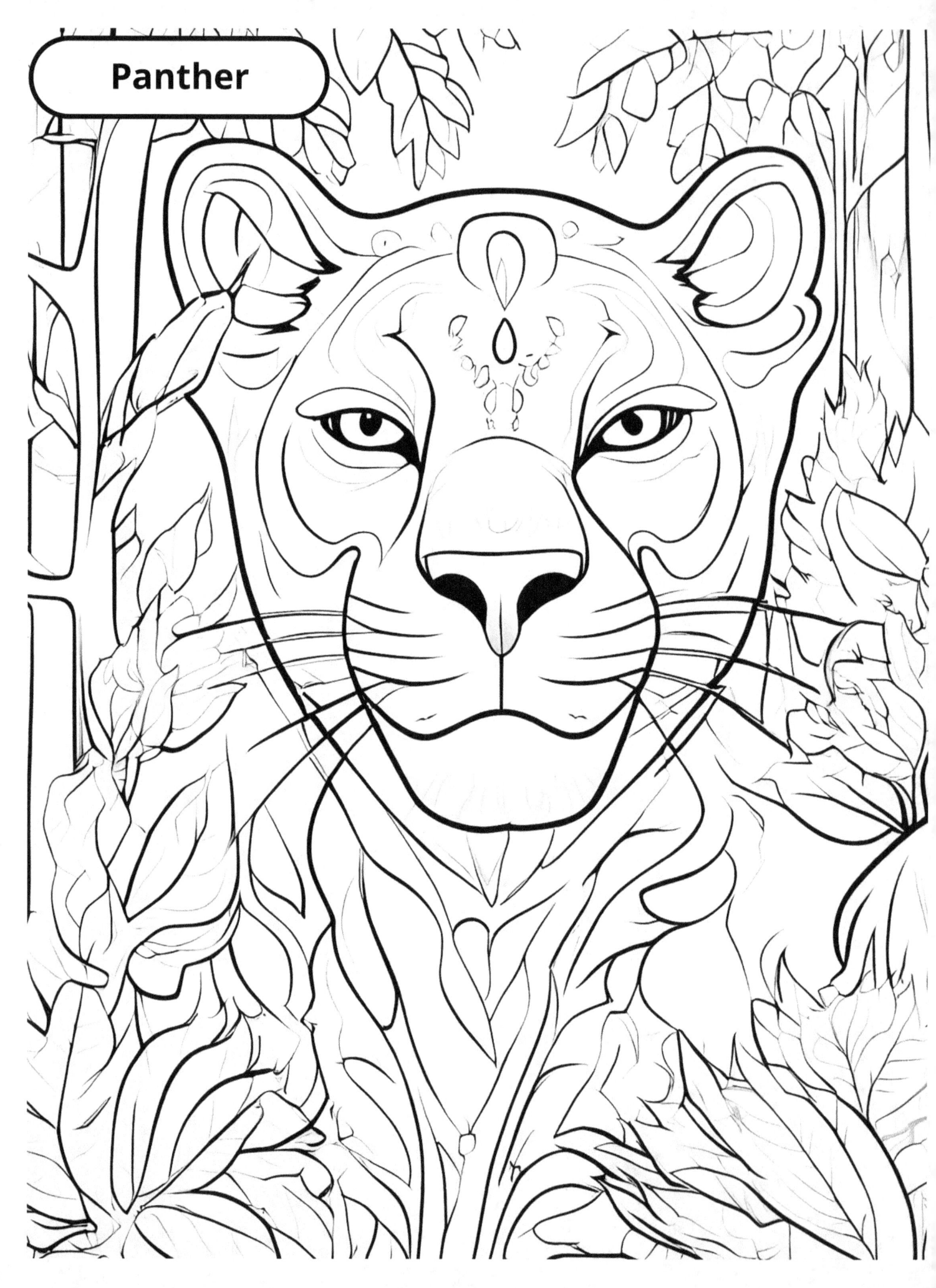

Panther

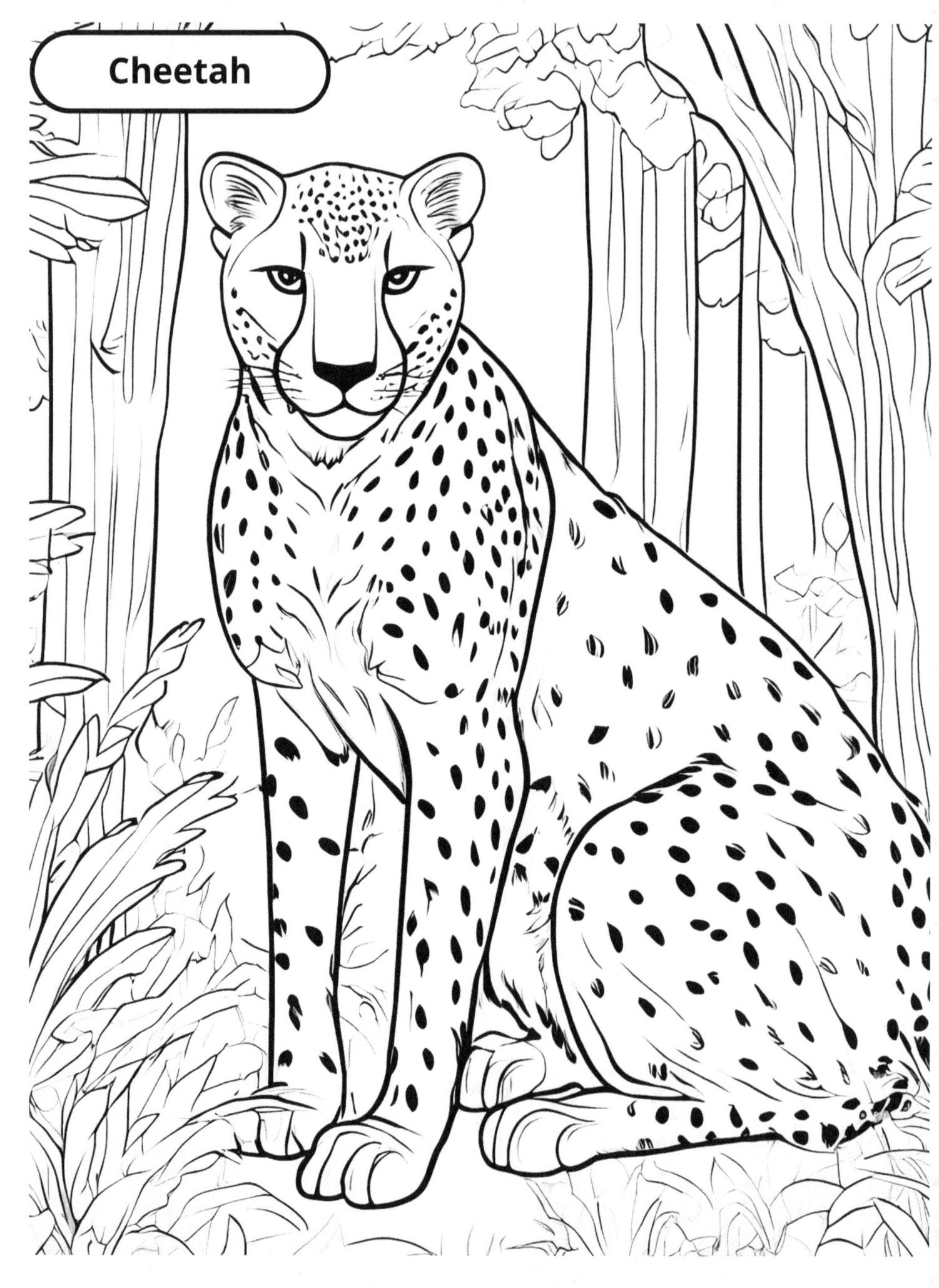

Cheetah

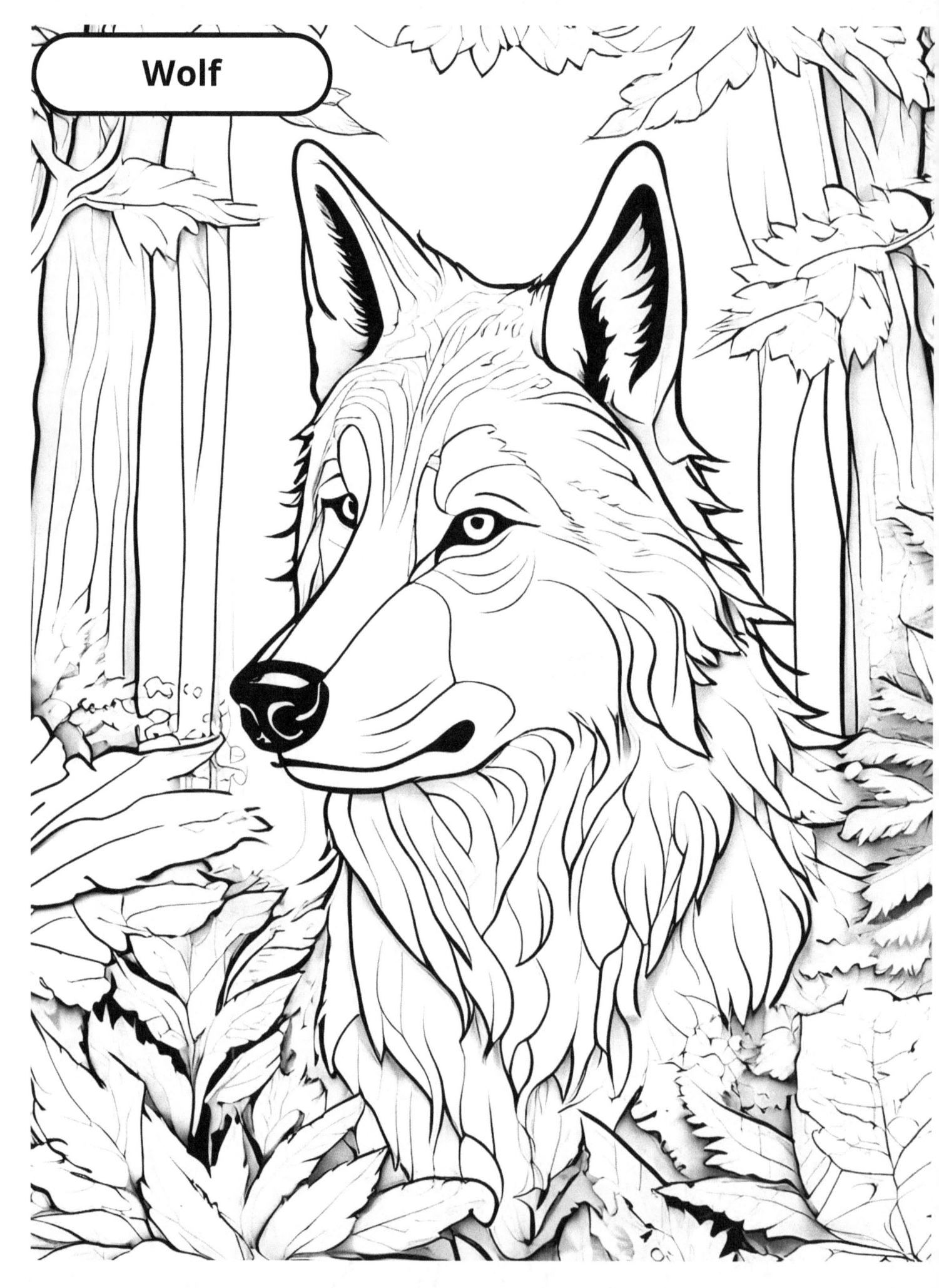

Wolf

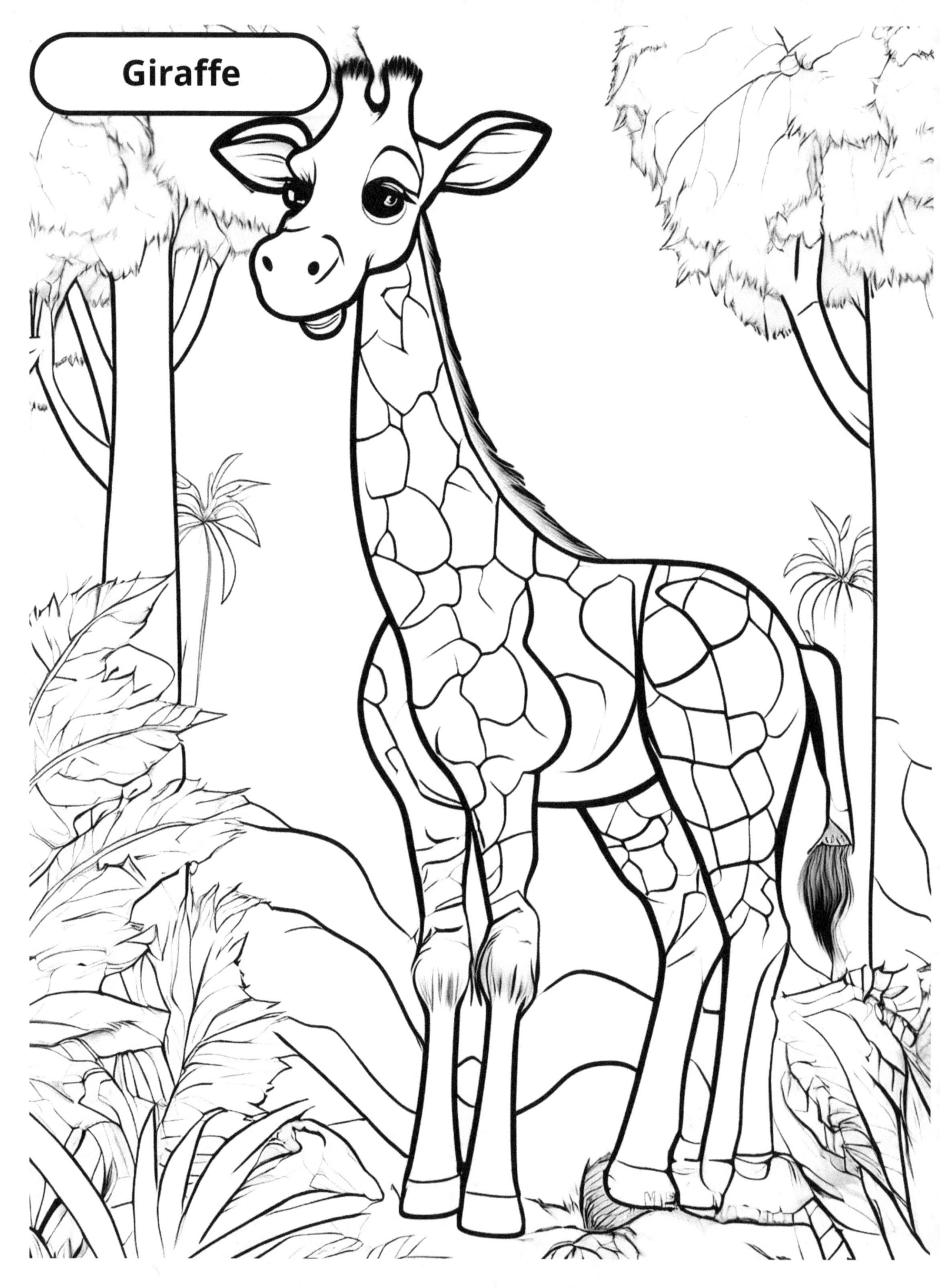

Giraffe

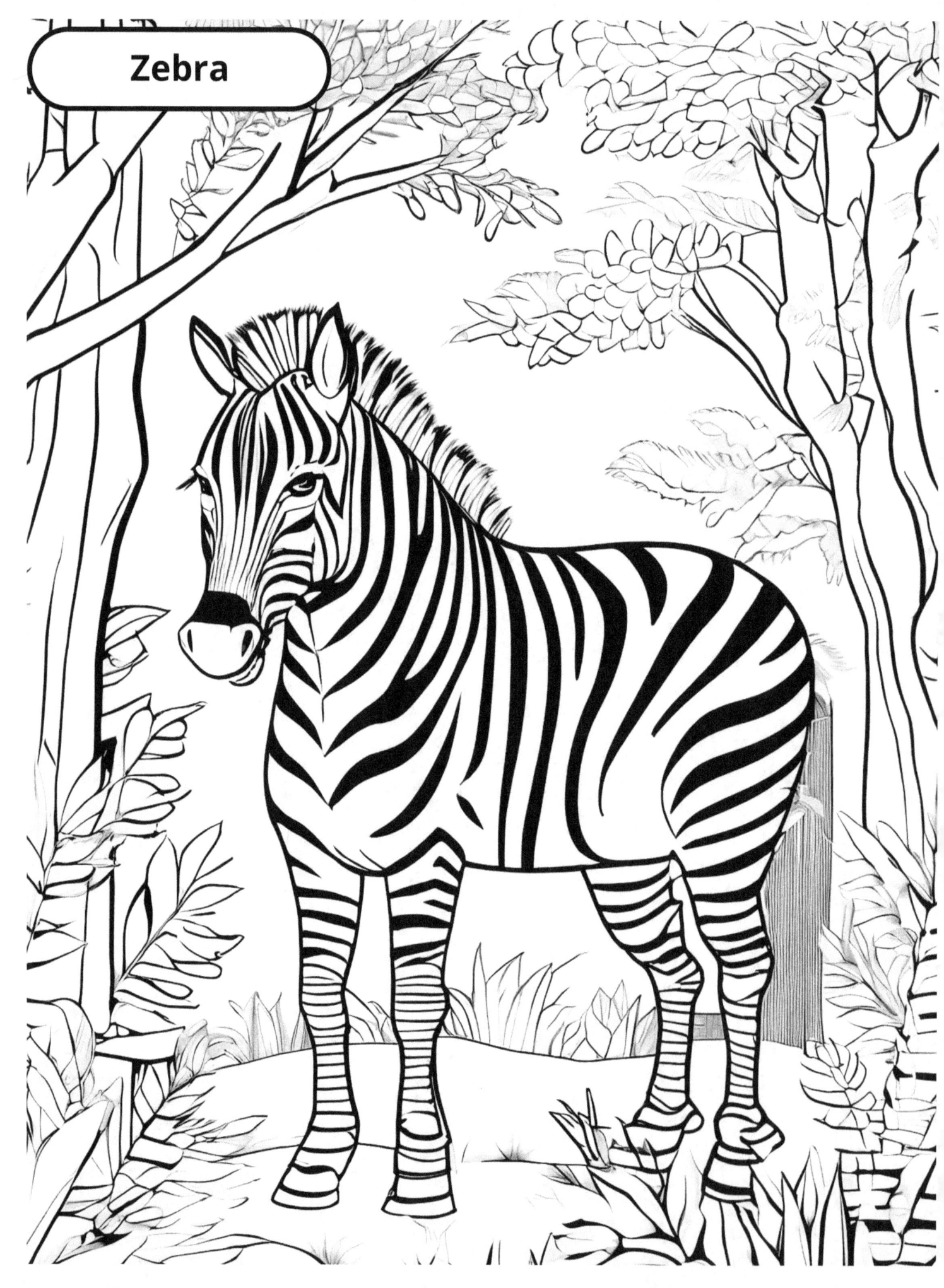

Zebra

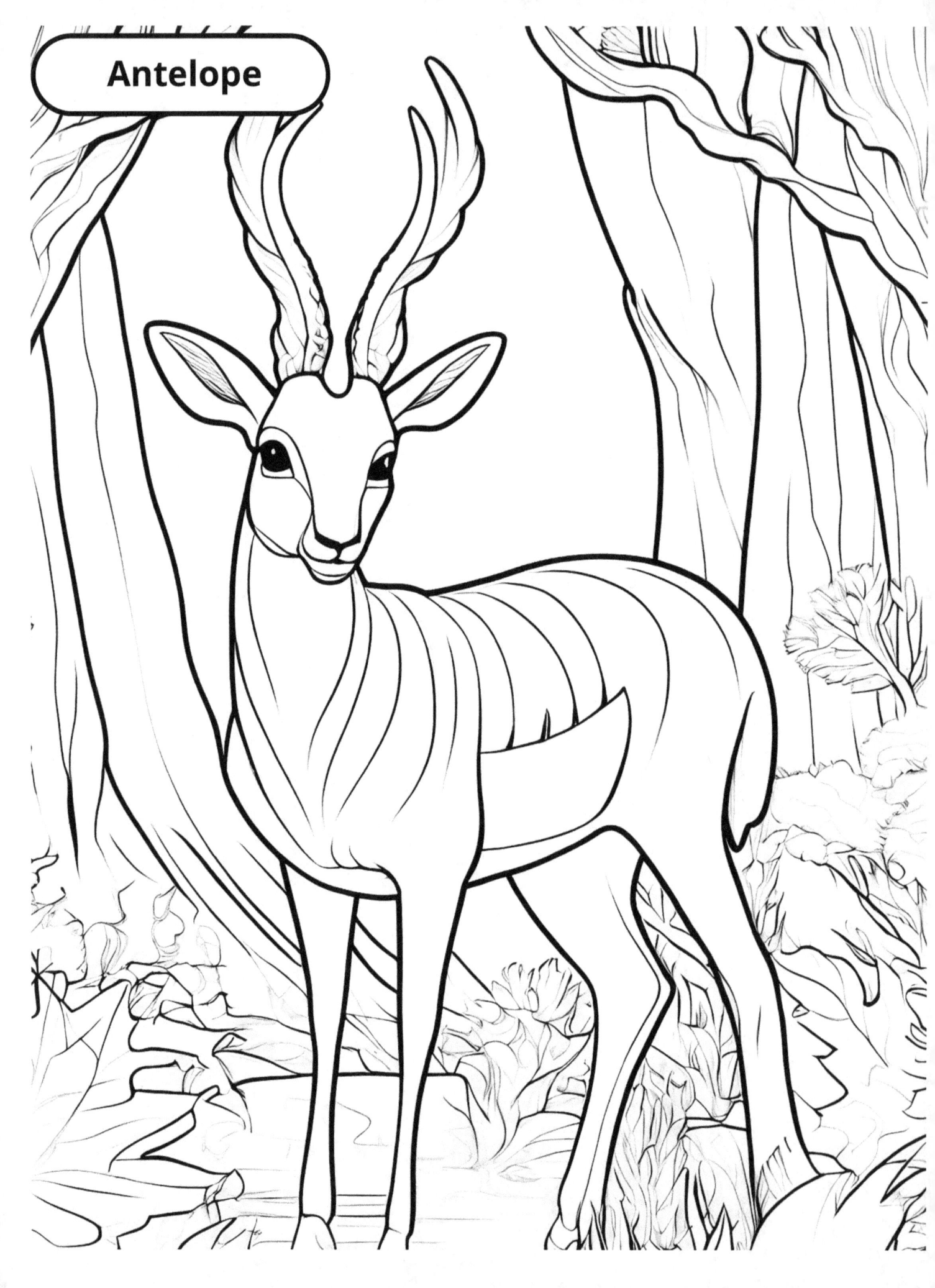

Antelope

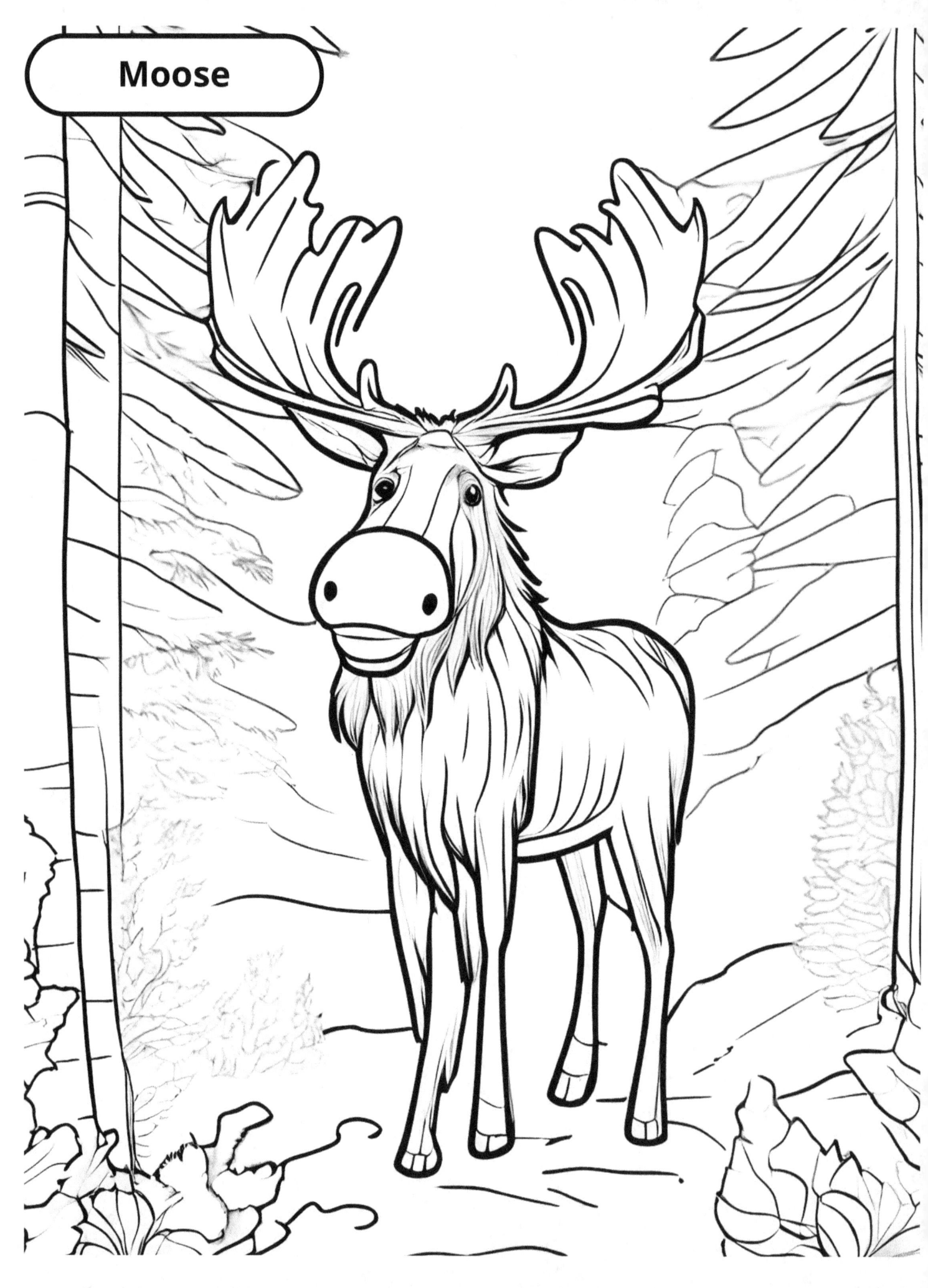

Moose

Elephant

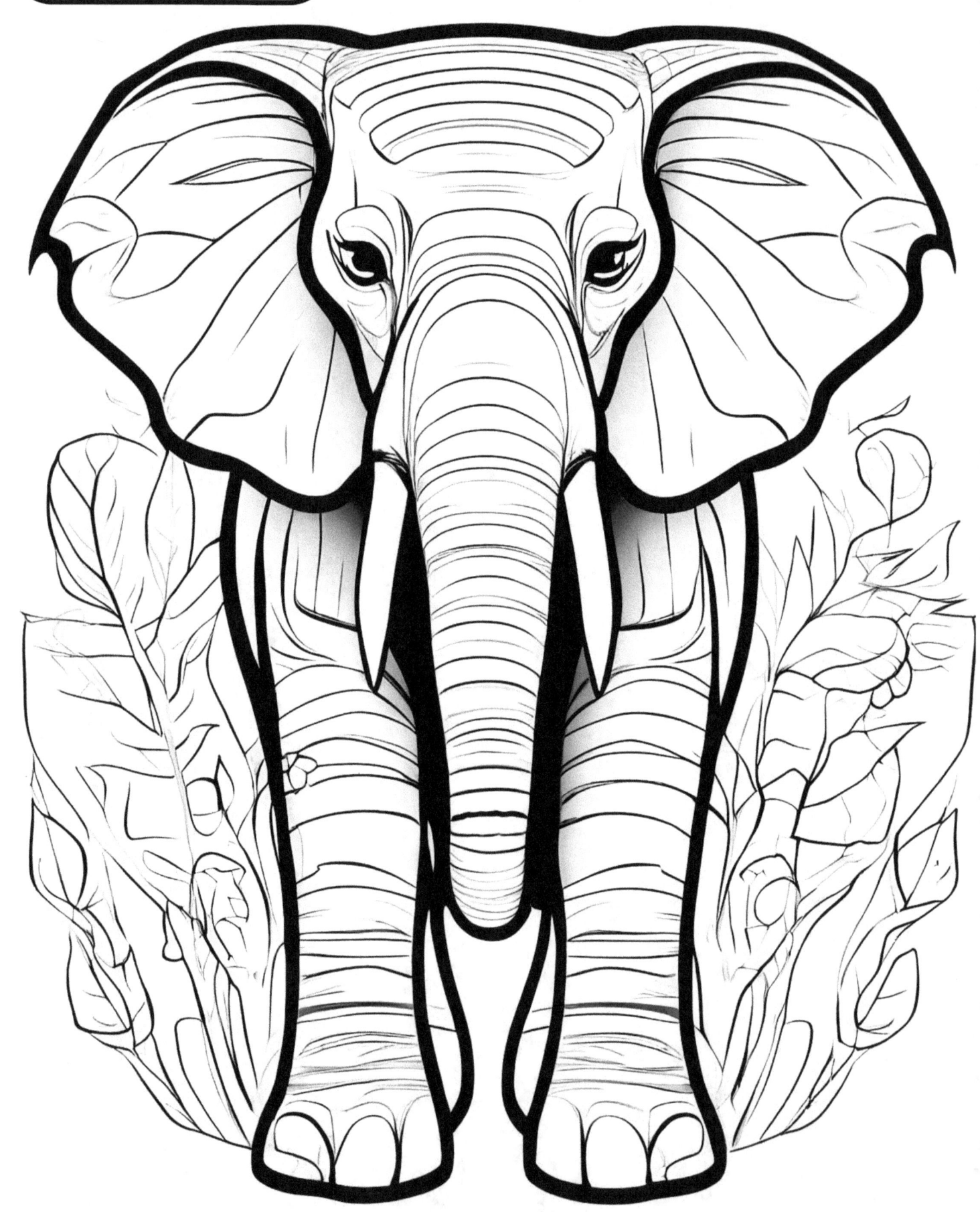

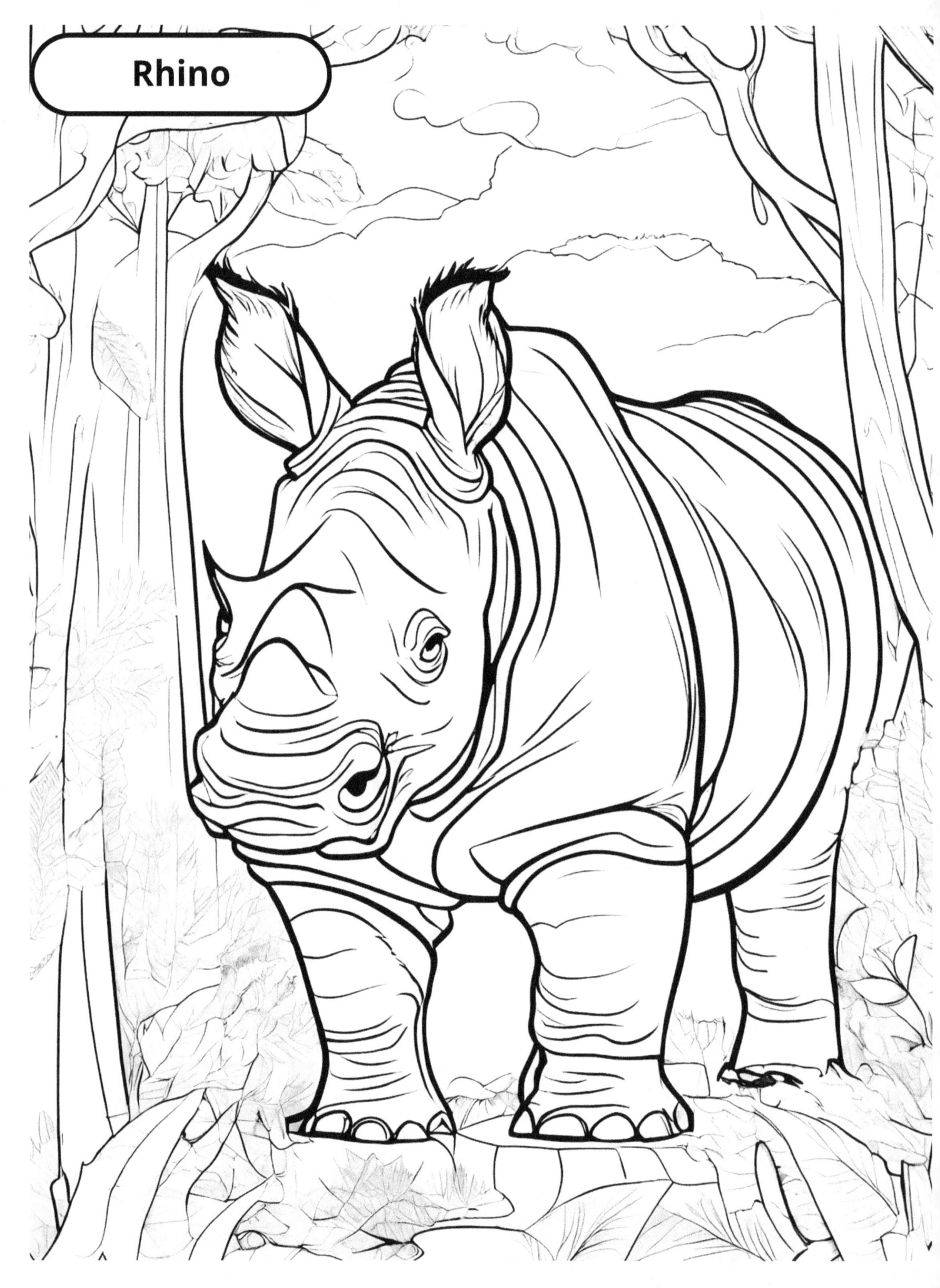

Rhino

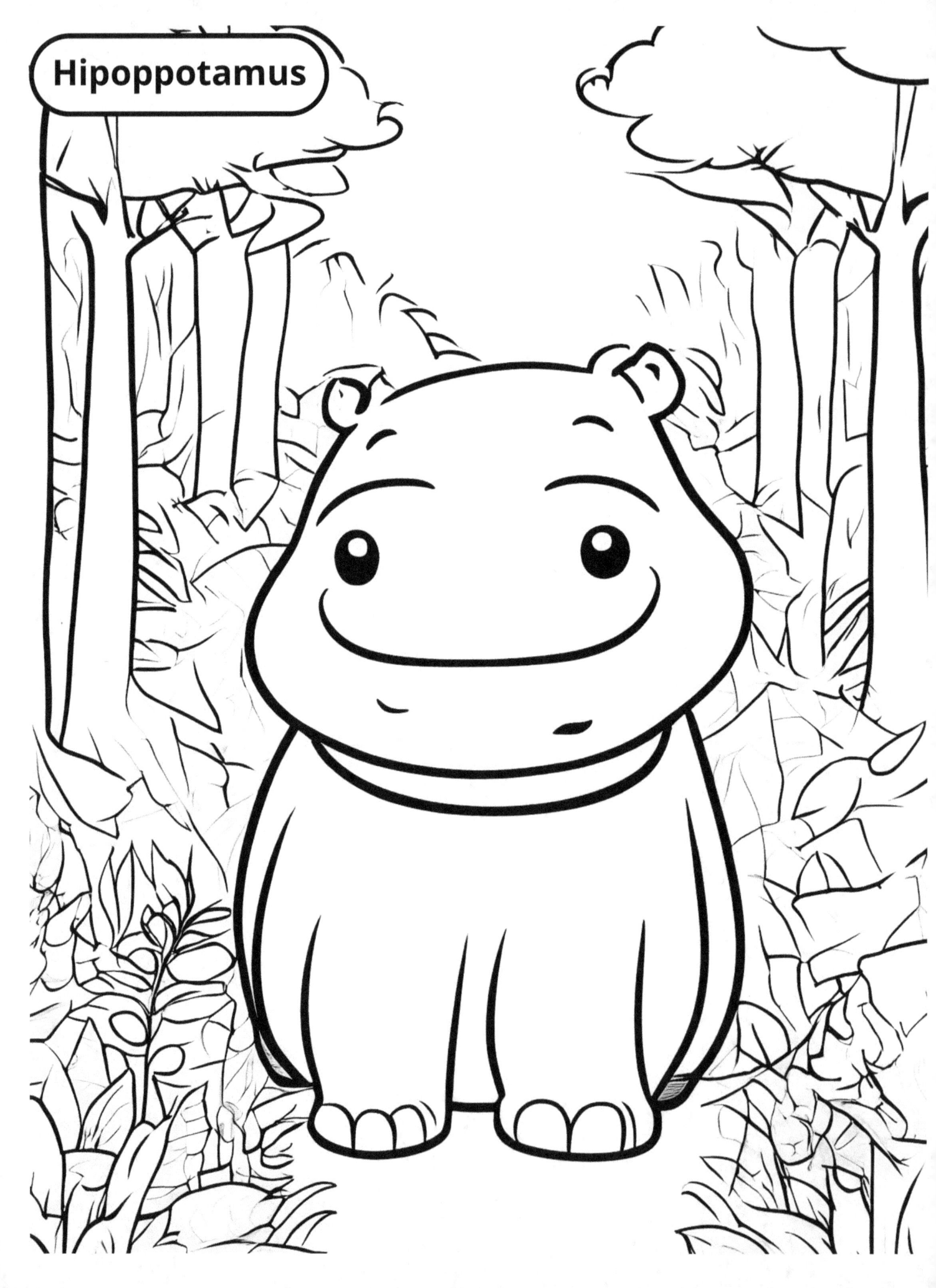

Hipoppotamus

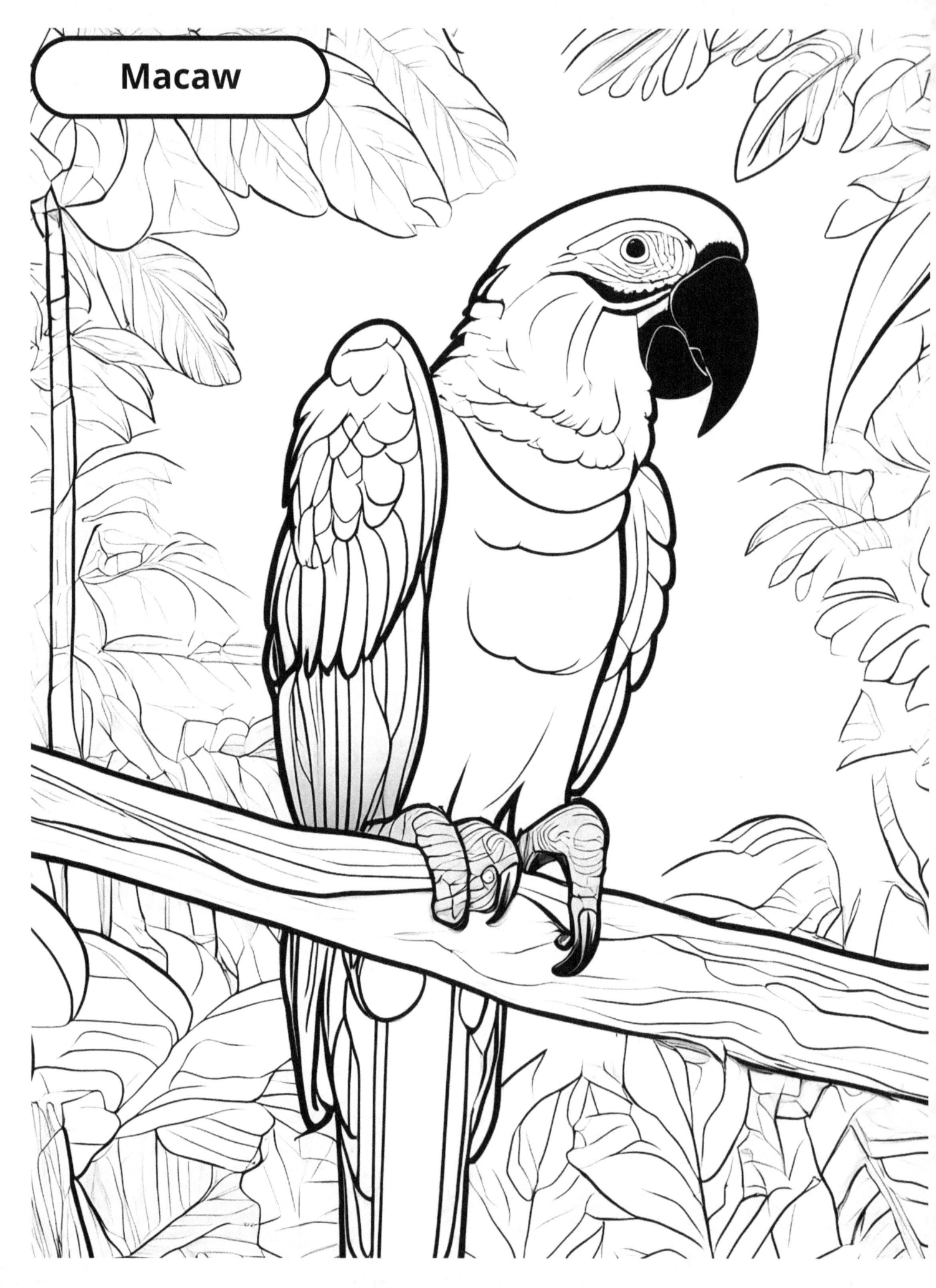

Macaw

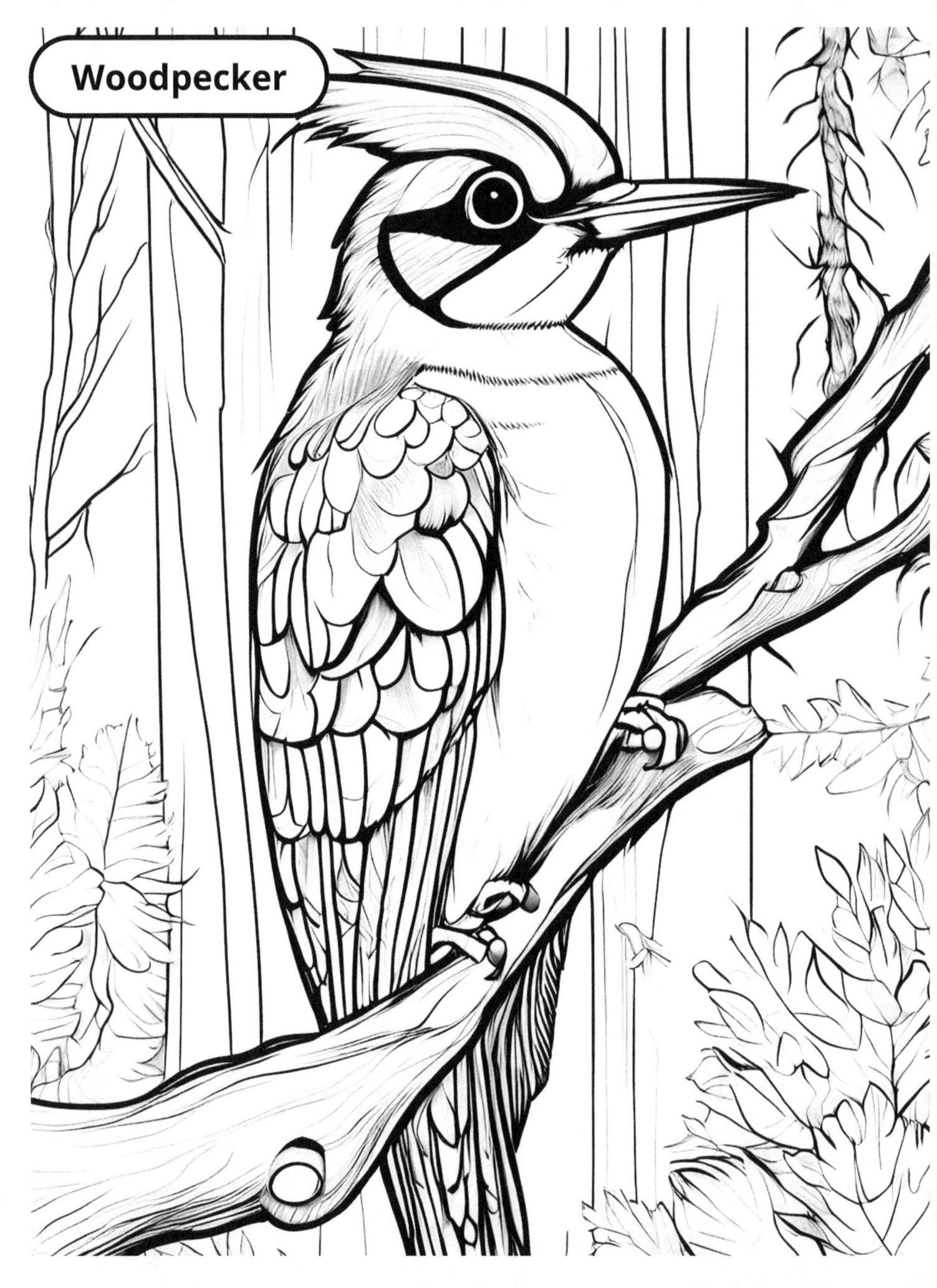

Woodpecker

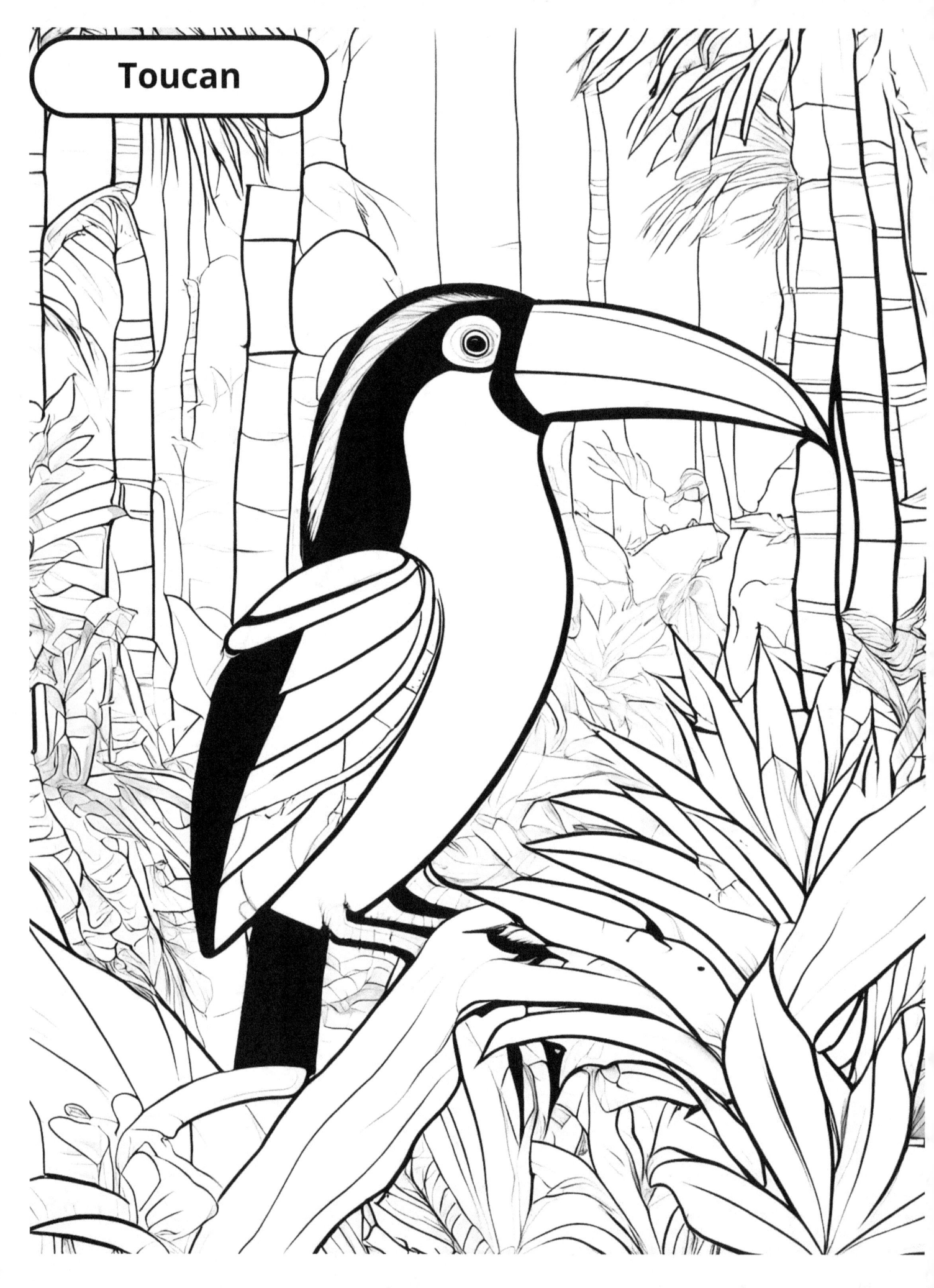

Toucan

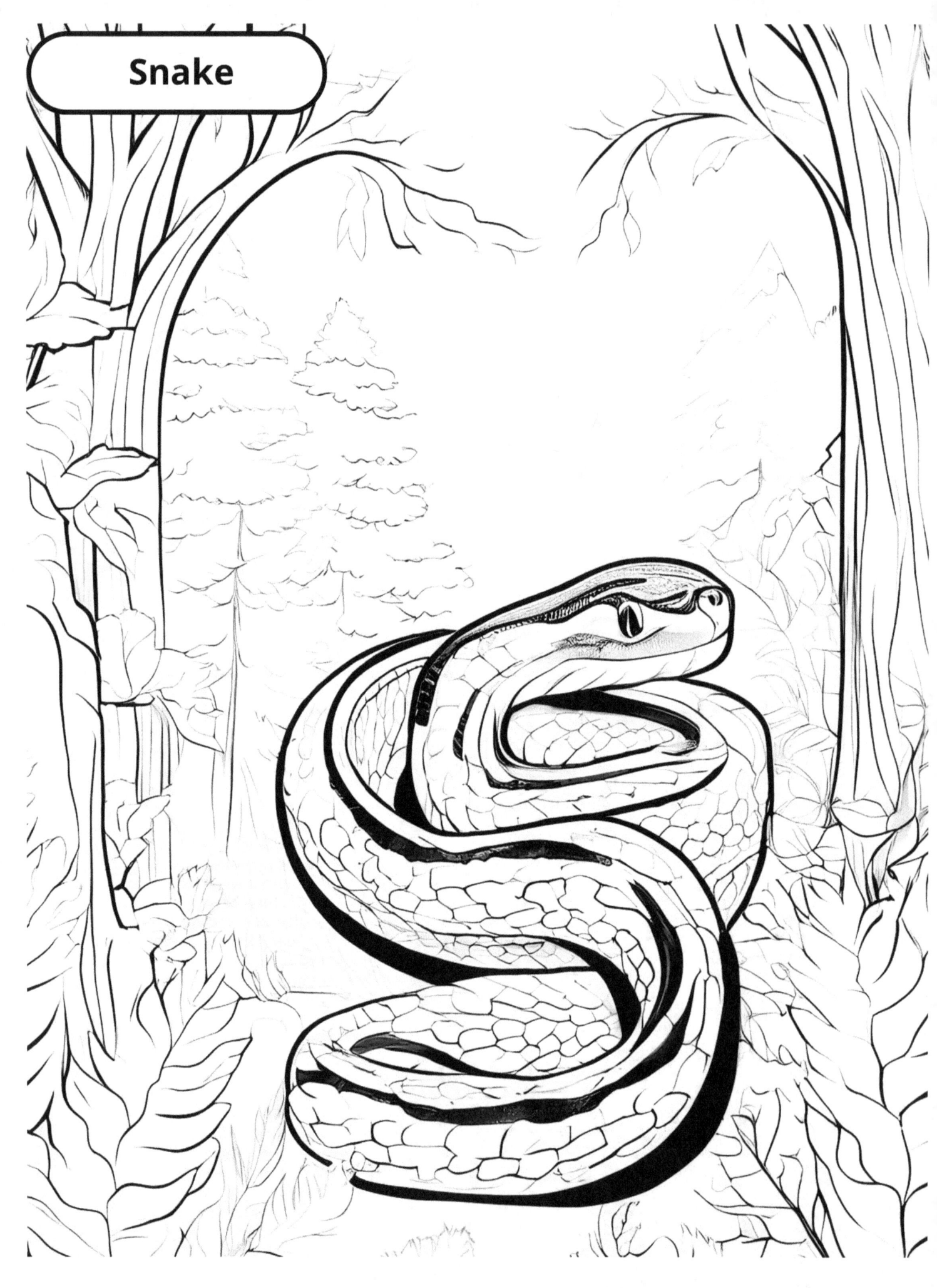

Snake

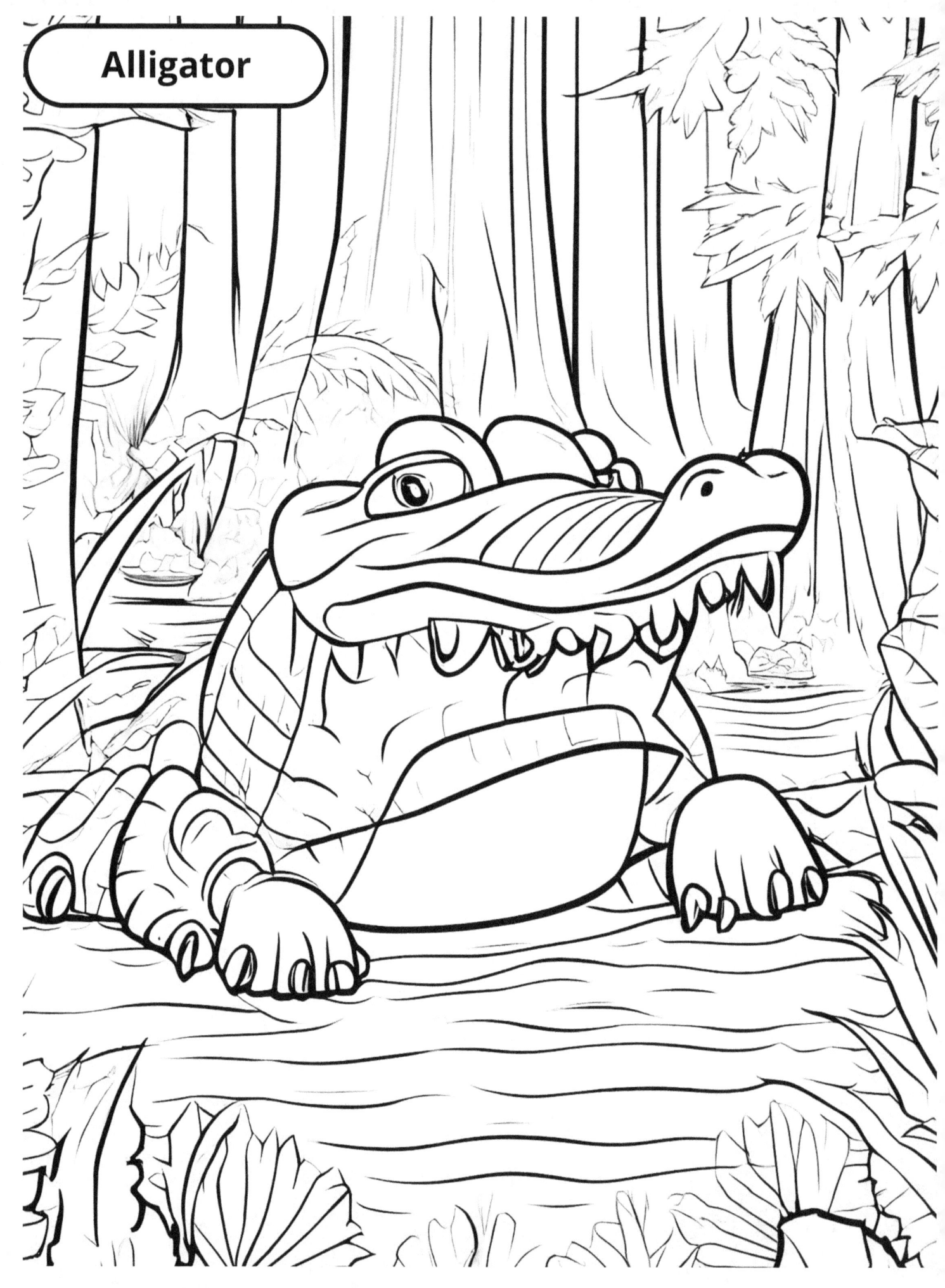

Alligator

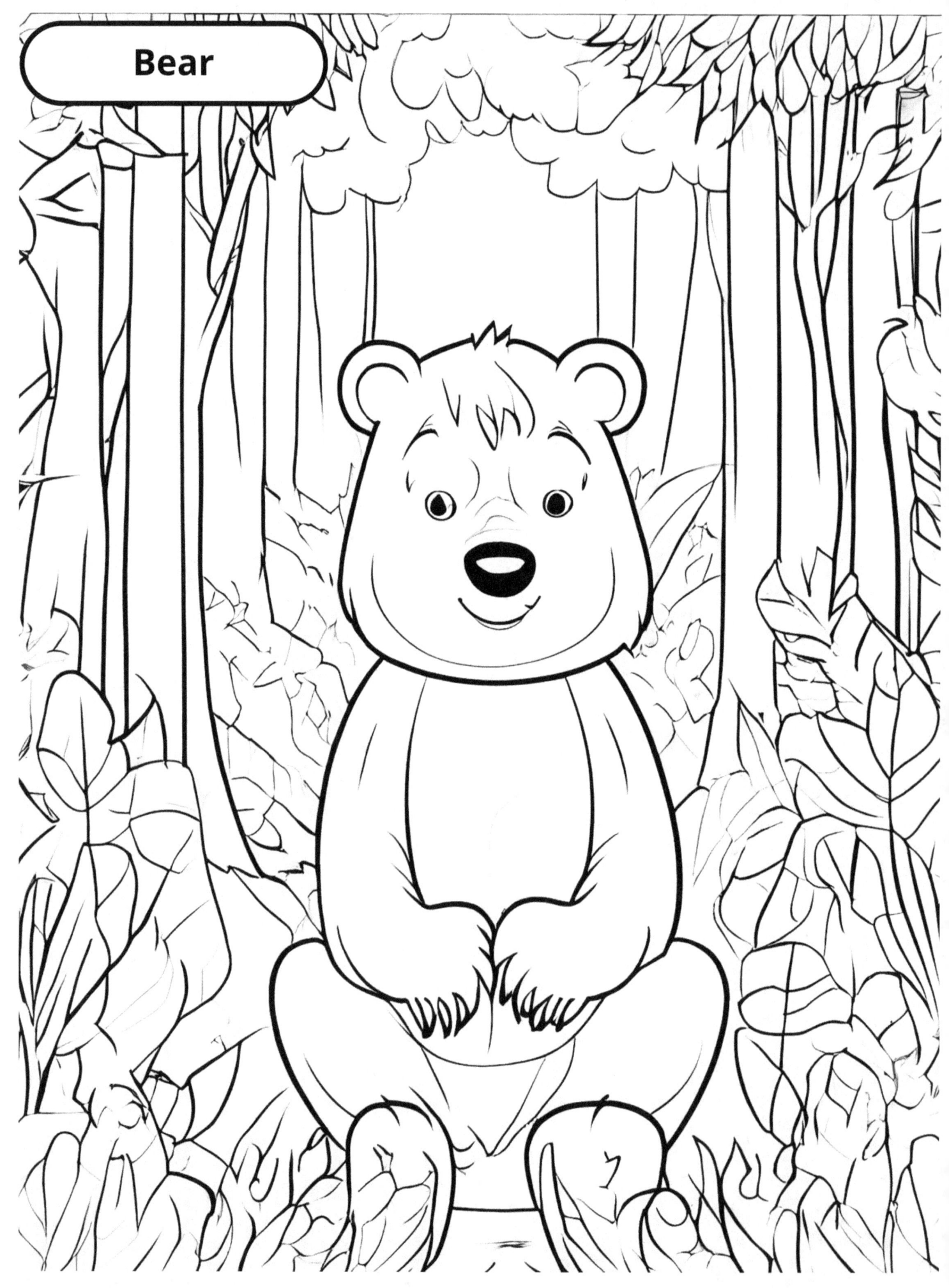

Bear

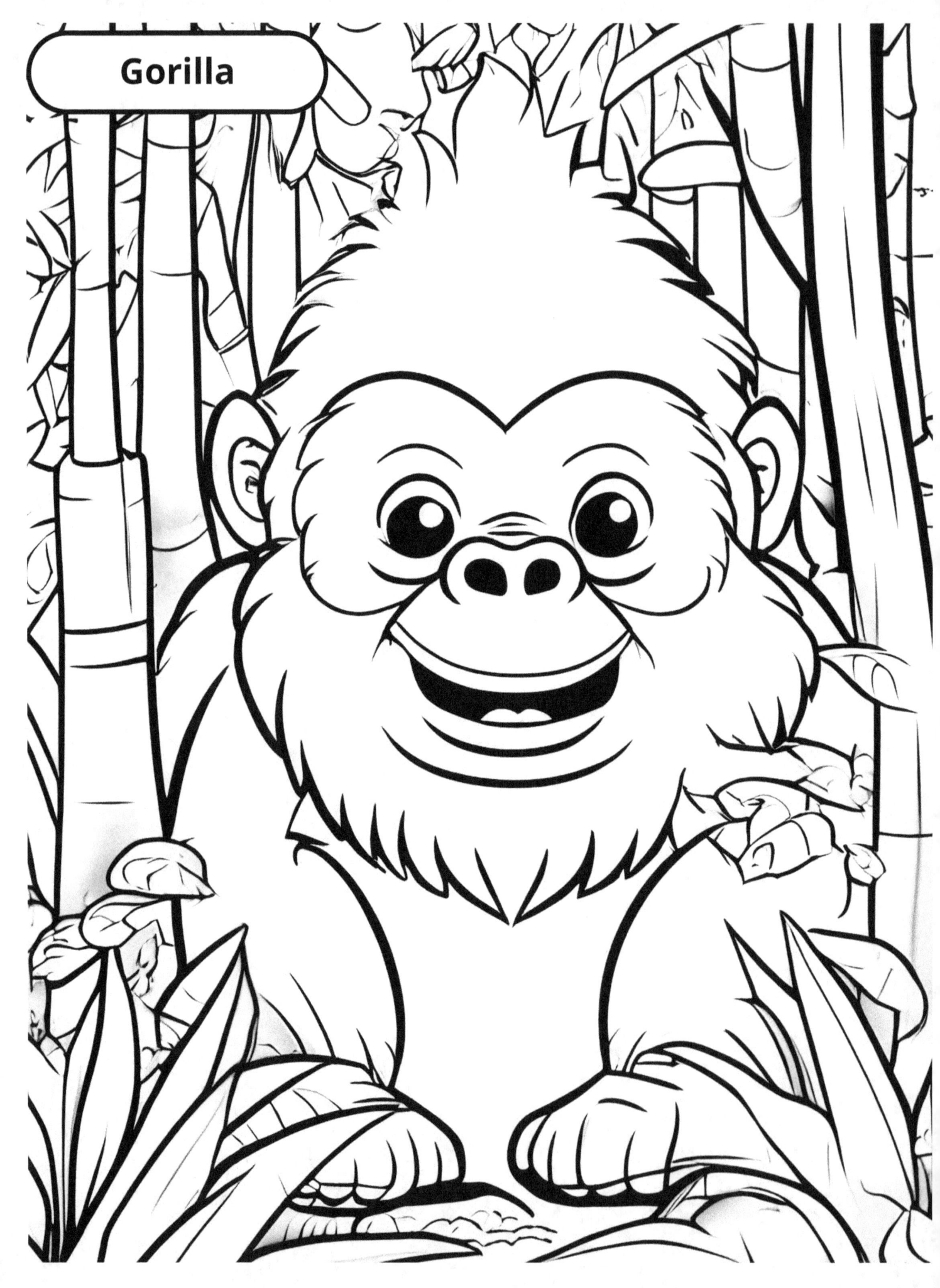

Gorilla

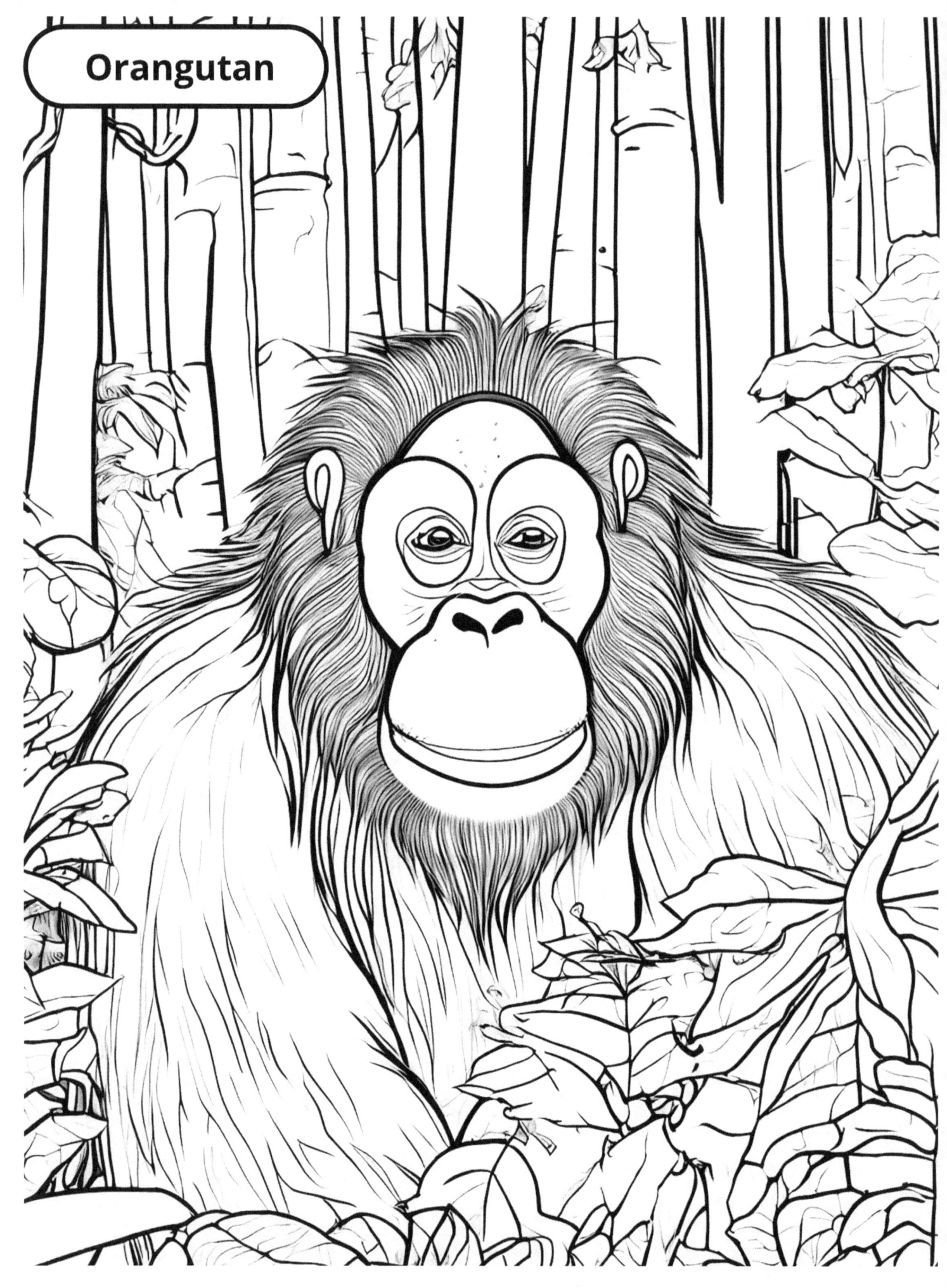

Orangutan

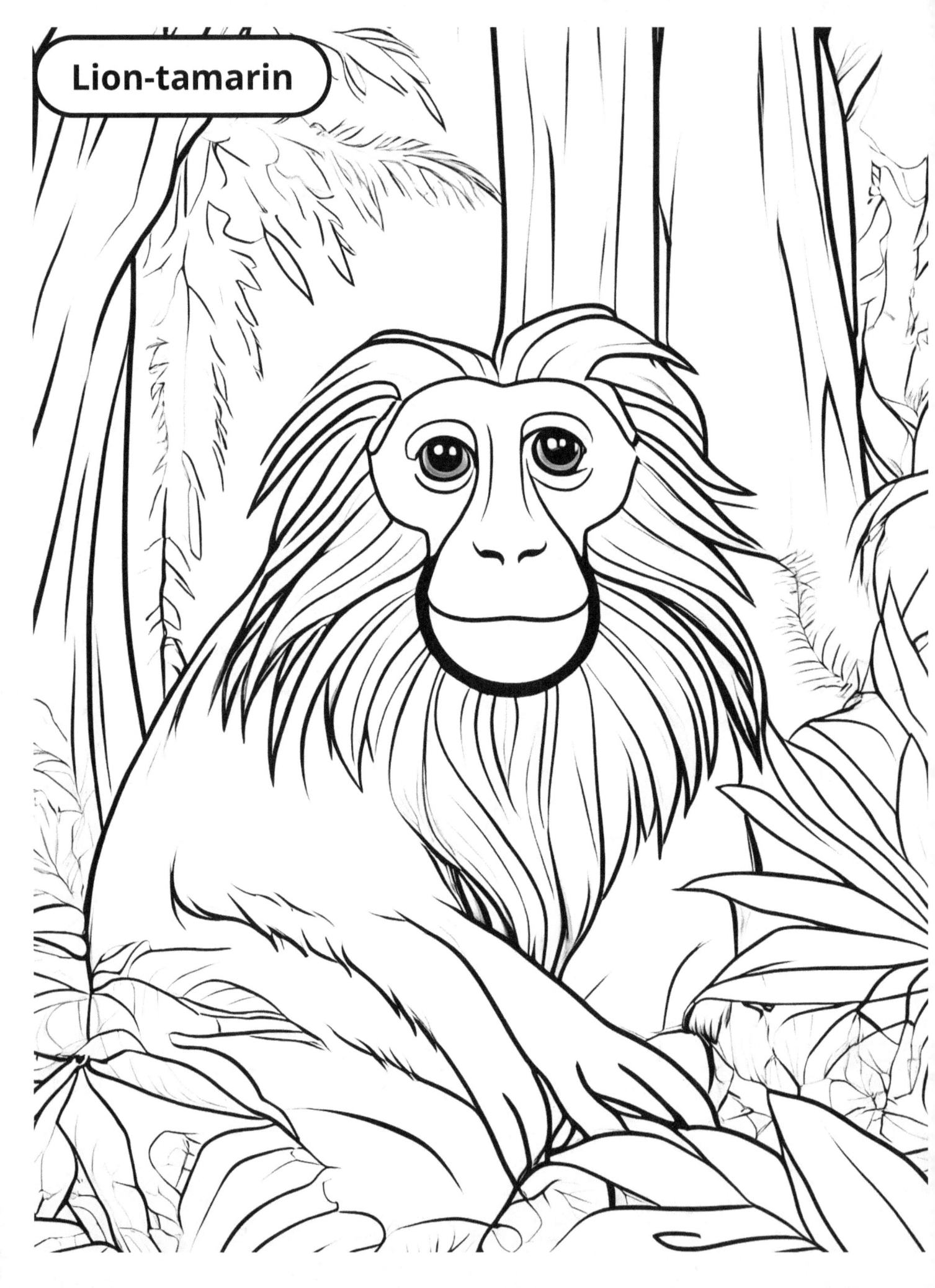

Lion-tamarin

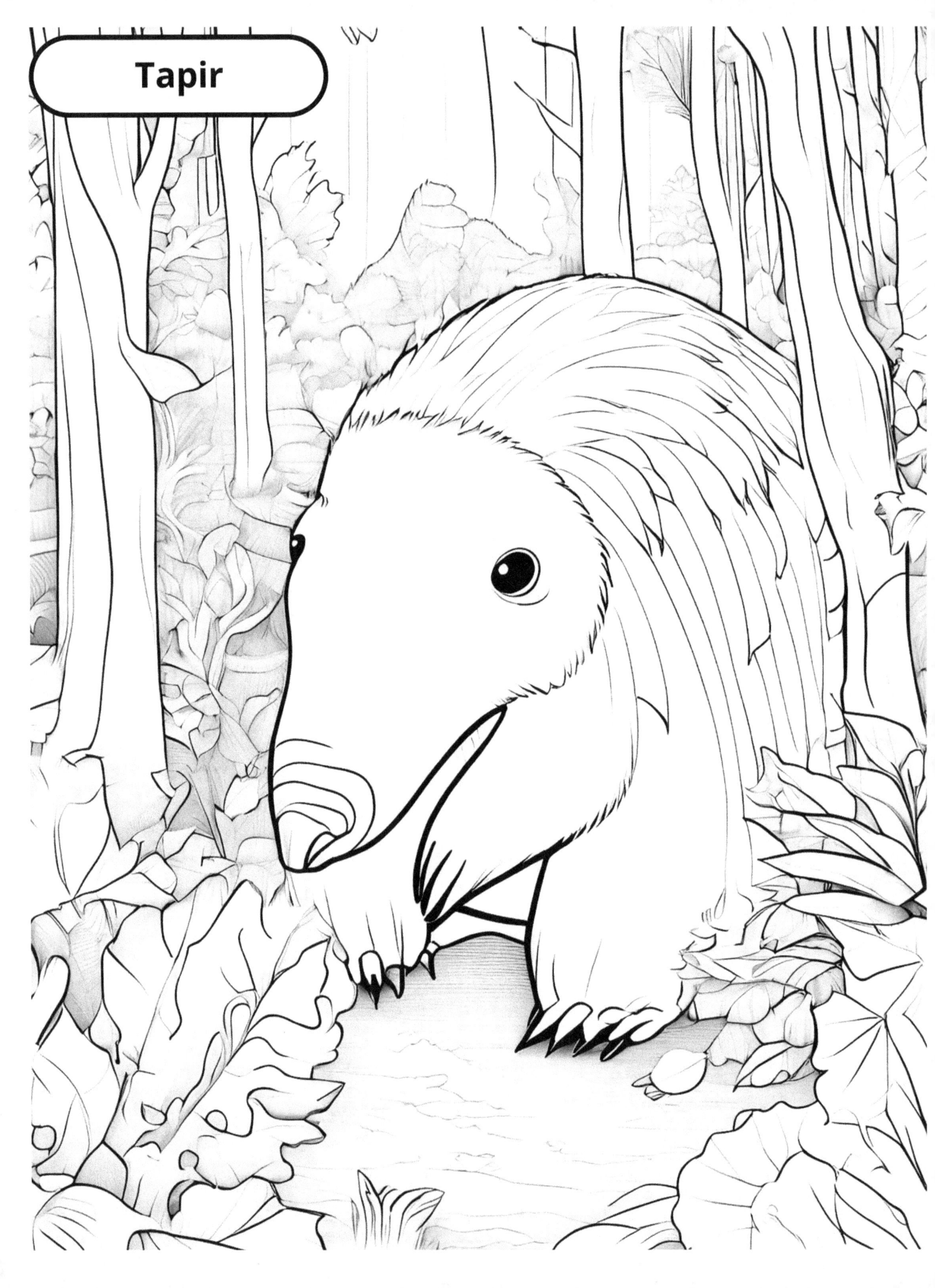

Tapir

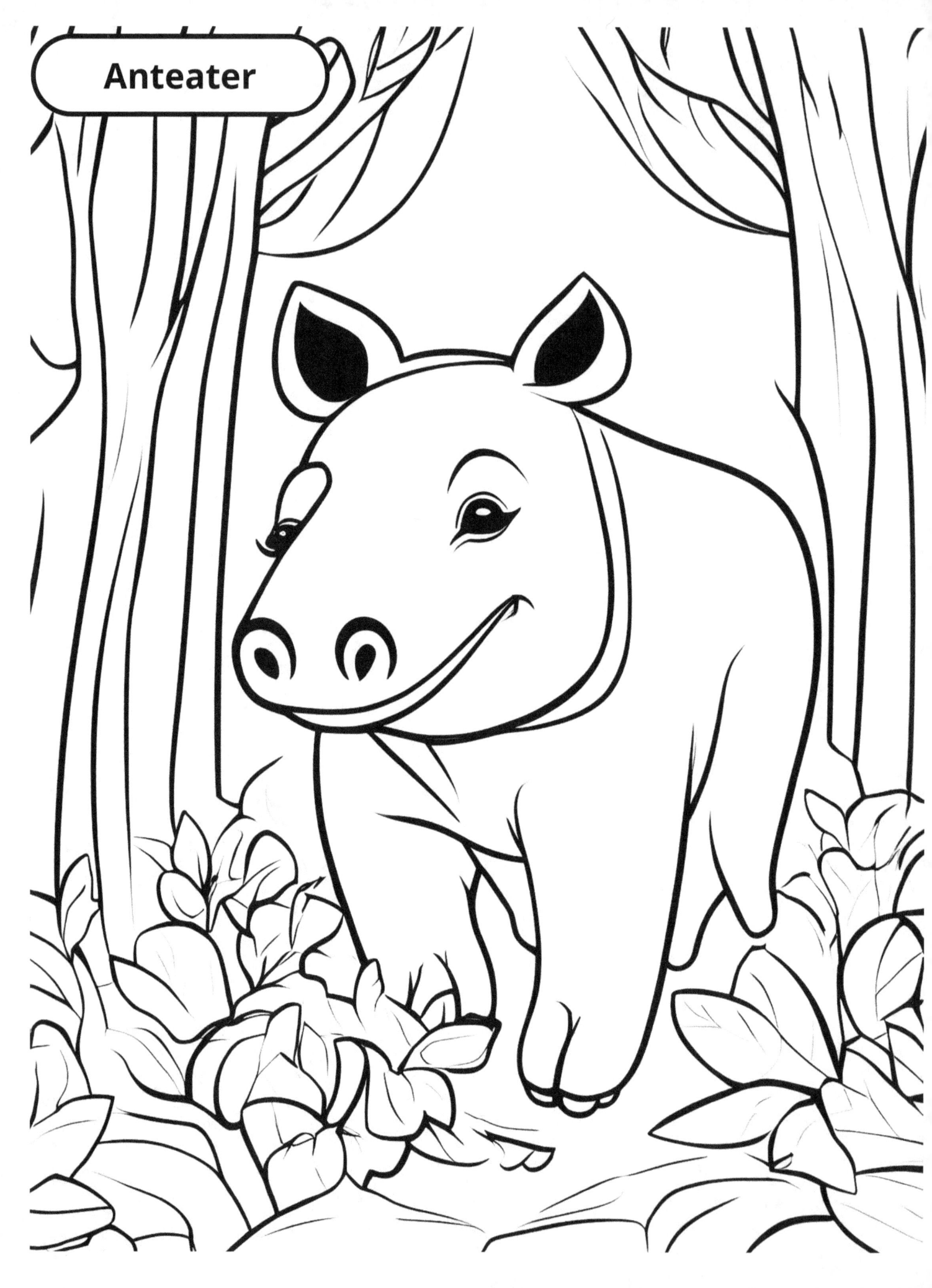

Anteater

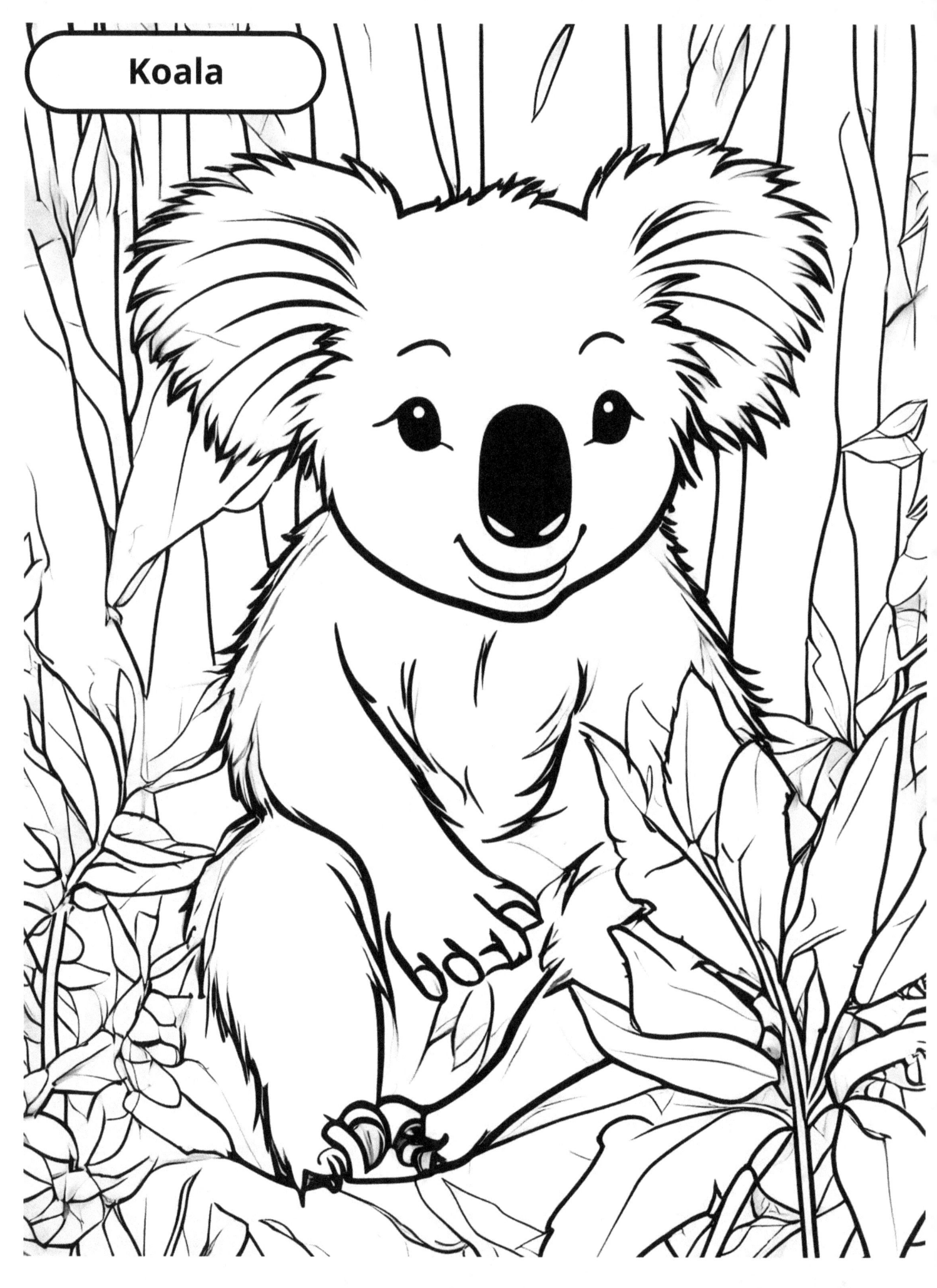

Koala

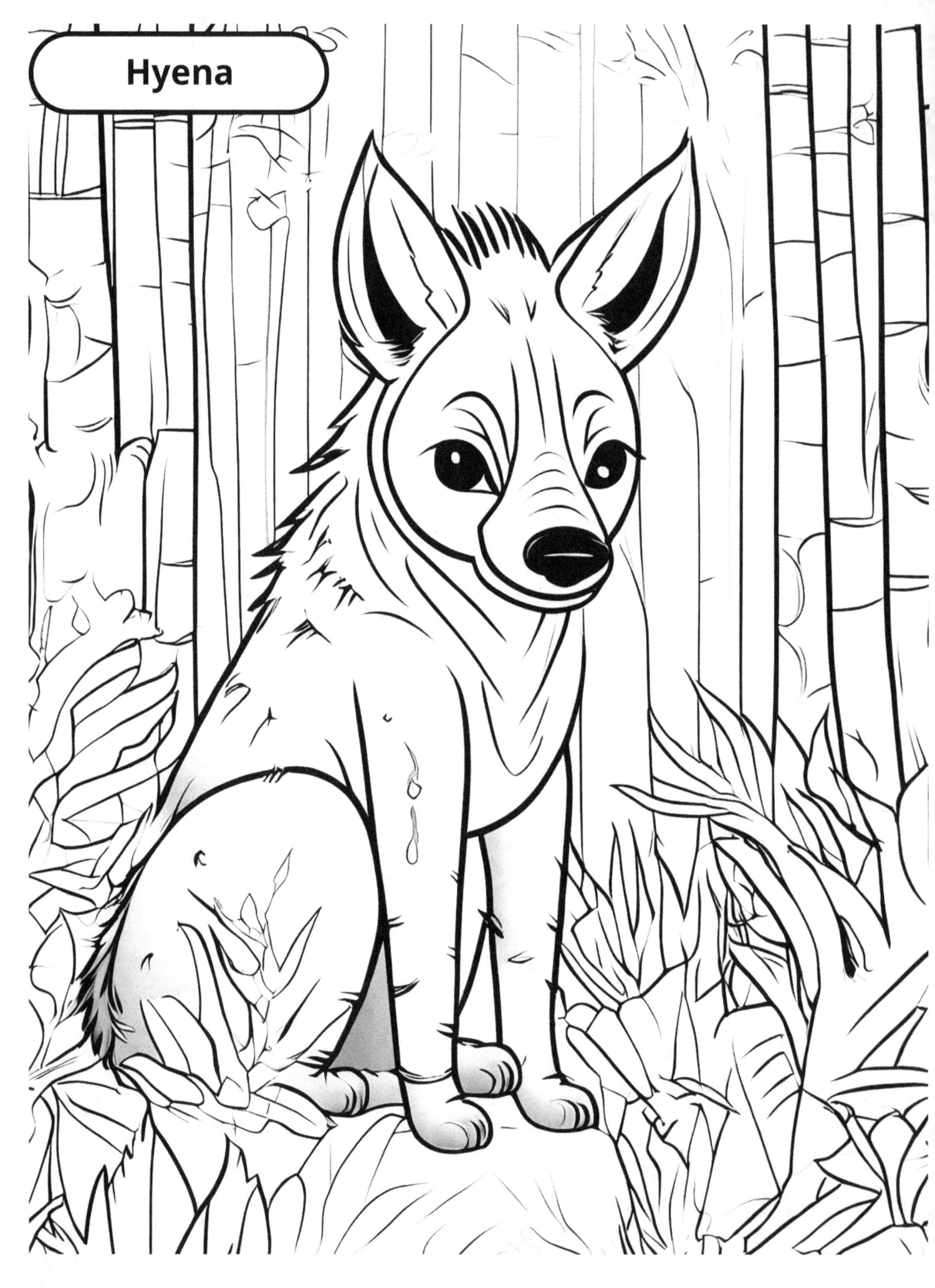

Hyena

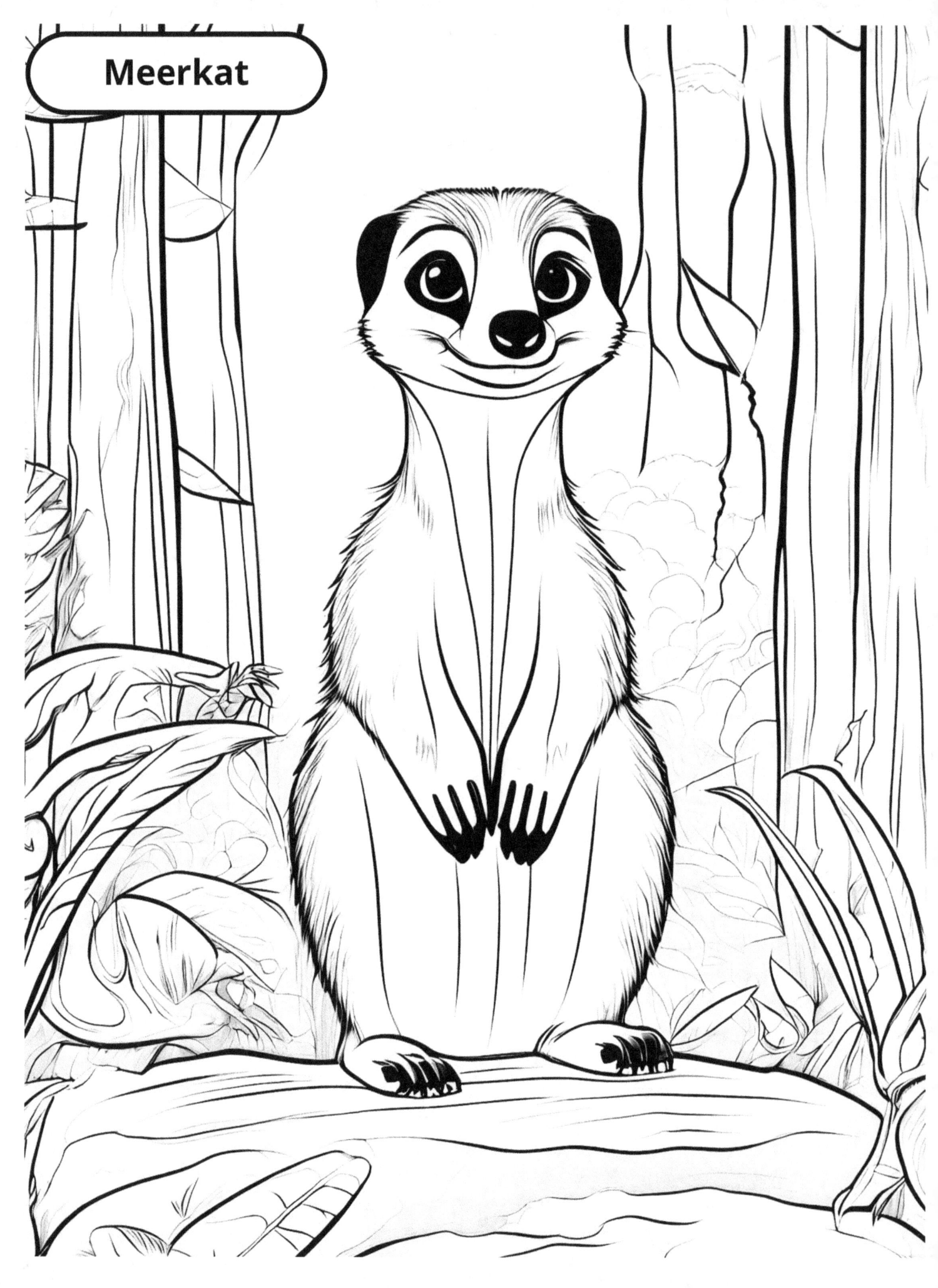

Meerkat

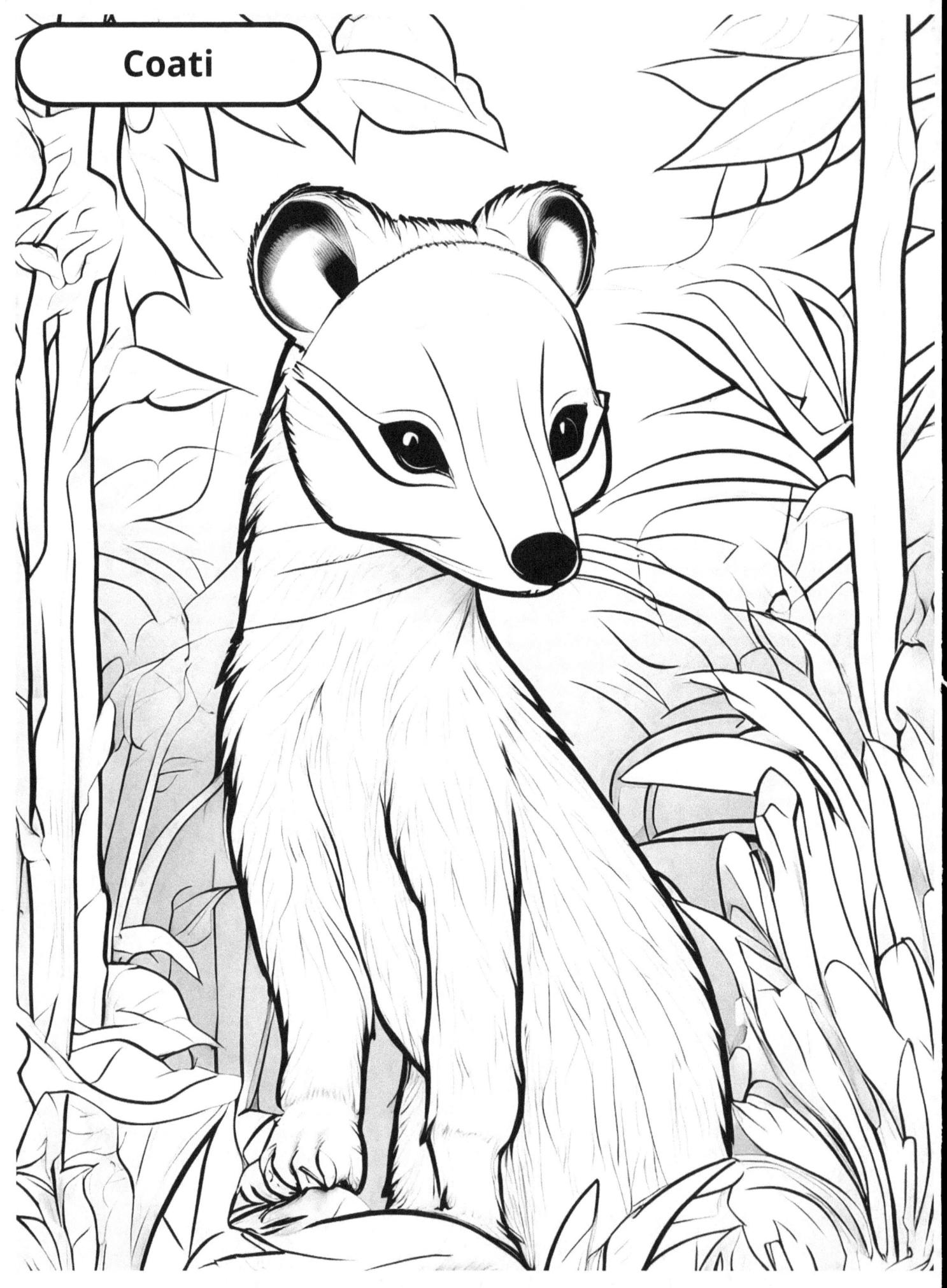

Coati